the VOICE of the MASTER

EVA BELL WERBER

DEVORSS & COMPANY, PUBLISHER
BOX 550, MARINA DEL REY, CALIFORNIA 90294

Eighth Printing, 1988

ISBN: 0-87516-105-7

Printed in the United States of America

How can I speak — unless you listen?
How can you listen, unless you become still?
"Be still and know."

CONTENTS

THE VOICE OF THE MASTER

THE VOICE OF THE MASTER

THIS BOOK

TRULY I AM the door by which you enter the garden of this book. There wrapped in the warmness of My love, you shall abide, while I bring you lessons and truths which I would have you know. I invite you to walk in this garden of love with Me, letting Me guide and direct you, showing you the beauties of a life lived from My high point of consciousness. Sometimes we shall not even talk together, but rest quietly in sweet communion, drinking deep of a holy peace. As you put into daily practice the truths which I bring you, this garden of beauty will become very real to you and you will accept your heritage as a child of the King and abide forever in the safe shelter of My love. So—shall we step forth together? Read each day some little part, then go forth, putting its teachings into practice in your daily life and affairs, and you may prepare to accept the blessings which will pour upon you, from my full storehouse.

ENTER THE GARDEN

The Garden of the Heart is sheltered from the clamor of the world. It is a sweet and hallowed spot. There is a high wall as of a mighty flame about it. As you enter all that is unreal, all that is of the outer realm is burned away, and you enter the garden of your heart as pure spirit. You must drop from your feet the dusty sandals of worldly thought and the cloak of old consciousness will fall from your shoulders, for these things could not go with you through that wall of flame; but the flames do not touch the soul.

In an instant's turning of the thought back within you, severing it from the things of the outer realm where men function in work and play, you can be within this garden of reality, away from the world of *illusion*. There as in another realm, we walk together, and you learn from me the lessons of higher truth which I can give in no other way. You find rest and peace for your soul and refreshment for your physical body to draw upon as you again take up the tasks before you.

As you go from this lovely Garden of peace and stillness, you shall go forth with the sign of it upon you, and as you serve, you will carry a glow more radiant than the sun. You will be calm and poised through all circumstances for you shall not again put on the dusty sandals, nor the musty robe, but shall don the new robes of higher consciousness.

EACH MUST ENTER ALONE

I hear you say, "Lord there are those I love whom I would take with me into this Garden of the Heart. I cannot leave them behind in their consciousness of despair, their feeble understanding, and unhappiness of circumstances." I say to you, "You may bring them to the very gate, but each soul must enter the Garden alone. Each soul must choose for itself to lay aside the world-worn garments and go through the flaming wall into the Holy Presence. You shall lead them by the glow you carry, causing them to desire that which they see you have. You shall so radiate love to them that they *will* seek to find it for themselves, and through you many *will* indeed enter the Garden of the Heart. Many shall you meet these coming days walking that trail that leads to the Garden. They *will* ask you the way, and you shall be directed how to answer them. Fear not that you shall not answer them wisely and well for you speak not your own language as of other days, but the language of Him who waits in that place for all who would seek Him out.

THE PEARL OF GREAT PRICE

As a pearl of great price shall My word be hid in your heart. You will often go within and take from the golden jewel case that gorgeous gem. My word is power. It shall see you through insurmountable difficulties of the material world. You shall take it up and speak it forth, and walls of stone shall crumble before it. My Word is Love. It shall warm and protecet you. Everywhere you go, up and down the land, this pearl of love shall make the highways bloom about your feet. By its use you shall give forth Love to all you meet.

My Word is Faith. With it in your heart you shall never doubt your power. You shall move on to greater and yet greater works. You shall speak forth the word with a great knowing that whatever you will shall be fulfilled unto you.

So learn to grow still and wait, that this word of Mine, which is likened to the Great Pearl shall be made known unto you. This is the true secret of a life of fullness of joy and service, and is what I crave for you My Beloved. As I speak to you from the pages of this book, even so do I speak from your heart's center. Never doubt that My Word is meant for you, to guide you on your daily path. It shall bless you in joy and comfort you in sorrow, and truly our companionship be sweet as we journey on together.

SAFE SHELTER

I would have you become more frequently aware of me, recognizing my holy presence in all of your daily affairs. I am the all of you, all that is real and eternal.

Why do you seek the solution of your problems outside of yourself when you will find the Father's love and understanding within?

I wait to share your every thought and desire, though I must remain silent and apart until you recognize My presence. On occasion I call gently hoping that you will hear and answer My voice.

When you have found the safe shelter in Me, you will lose all thoughts of fear. All the outer circumstances of your life will be a true reflection of that perfection dwelling within you.

Then will you live a life of security among the passing things of the world. Then we shall walk and talk untouched by the changes of time and limitation.

LISTEN TO THE VOICE WITHIN

When you seem to have strayed away from Me, when the busy days have followed one after the other, with only snatched moments of high contact, you need not feel that you need beseech or implore Me to return unto you. You need not do a penance. No Beloved, you have but to turn within in love and adoration for there I wait, there I have always been. It is within that you shall come and find that the sweetness you have missed has always been there, has always been waiting for you to take it. My love is freely given and I wait patiently for you to come and receive. My strength is there for you to come and use. Come My beloved, as the golden flame of the candle burns so steadily and sure, just so steady and so sure is my strength and love burning there within the secret place of your heart. Why depend on human strength or understanding when within your own being is that which is perfect, which has always been a part of you and has had no beginning and shall have no ending. Pause, listen to the voice within, then go forth to walk in sweet communion, doing the tasks that lie so close at hand; doing them with the strength and joy of the Almighty burning high within you. Then shall these tasks that await your doing be easily and happily done. The hours shall move smoothly and you shall find such joy in the celestial companionship that you enjoy that you shall indeed not labor and shall truly know that the Father indwelling works through the human vessel.

EXPRESSION

As my instrument, you go forth this day. Only through Man, the highest form of My creation, can the mighty works be carried on. So must you ever watch and pray that you see with clear vision and hear My voice as it guides and directs you.

Then what shall you fear, for as you thus serve Me, as I reflect perfectly through you, all your paths shall be those over which I would have you journey. All that comes into your life will be brought there by Divine direction. No circumstance shall you count other than good, and no fear need assail you. Only fear that you should shut yourself off from the Divine inflow, for then only could aught but good come your way.

At that point do I give you your choice. Walk with Me and have the glory of the Holy Presence shine all about you or walk alone and be amid confusion and at the mercy of the winds of circumstances and conditions. I yearn over those who should express me and through whom I might glorify the world in which they dwell. I long to give these My children riches of My kingdom and it is only because they will not accept themselves as a channel for My expression that all these woes and disturbances of the outer overtake them. So let us go together My child, this day, working, joyful, loving together, that I may give you My full measure of joy and gladness of heart.

COMPLETENESS

As eternity is without beginning and without ending, so am I, the One within you. All Knowledge is within, all love, all truth, all richness.

Why do men live and dwell in darkness when by turning inward in a moment of stillness, they can find waiting for their use, the glory of a life complete? Why do they struggle to demonstrate that which they already have? Does a man having a large vineyard run up and down the highway seeking for a vendor of grapes?

If you will but look up into the Father's face, saying, "Father, I thank Thee for what Thou art, and because Thou art all I need, my every need is met in my outer world of experience. As I contemplate Thy fullness of Being, knowing that I am a child of the loving Father, I too have all that the Father has."

I, the Father within you reflect My fullness, My completeness, My perfection through you, My human vessel of expression. You need fear no lack, disease, or distress of any kind. You need only to love and praise and give thanks and your life shall be a harmony of all that is lovely.

YOU DO WELL

As you sit at the feet of your Master, you do well, for He is Master of your life, even the breath upon which you subsist in physical form. You do well, for it is here that you learn of realities. Here you learn the beauty of meekness and the sweetness of love. Not the human love that longs to receive ere it gives, smothering the object of its affection with a closeness of personality, but you learn of a higher love which gives freely, thereby freeing all upon whom it is bestowed. Here do you find the richness of peace; and wisdom shall also enter your heart, that all through the coming days you shall walk wisely among your fellowmen.

So often have I *besought* you never to neglect these few moments alone with Me. Never substitute for this quiet time, another form of worship, no matter how worthy the form. I have so much that I can give in no other way. Be still, talk often with Me. Know Me in the sweetness of utter bliss. Then can My voice come to be heard amid the uproar of a mighty city as well as in the quiet of the mountain top at night.

Wait now, for I would fill and enfold you in My loving strength and after thus waiting go forth as a lighted candle and all shall follow the gleam you carry as you go your way.

REST

Rest my child. Rest in My tender arms. Feel the comfort flowing into your soul and the strength into your body. Need there be always words between us? The world is full of chatter. Can we not come just quietly together, you, brought only by a sense of need for comfort and stillness amid the tumult of life's activity, and I feeling the desire to pour My great Love and tenderness out to one of My beloved.

And so we meet in the sweet stillness and you feel the warmth of Me enfolding you and the things which mattered so greatly a few moments ago seem far away and of little consequence. Here there is only stillness, and sweetness and rest. Then with a smile upon your lips you arise and go again about the daily tasks. No word has been spoken by either, yet you are so filled with the Presence that all your being is aglow and life begins anew while you sing its harmonies throughout the commonplace duties of the day.

COME TO ME

Unless you come to Me I cannot help you. I must stand silent and yearning until you come and put your hand in Mine. So gladly would I enfold you in My love, so much would I give to you of My wisdom, that you might in turn give it forth to others of My children. I would not chide you thus, did I not see in you a sense of fear and need, and a wondering if after all I care for My own, or if only chance rules your days.

Listen! Breathe deep of my heavenly perfume. Be still. Know that only the personal self of you can get in the way, and keep the plan of your life from being fulfilled. Put down that personal self with its fears, its beliefs, its opinions, and be once more as a simple child, walking with its hand clasped by the hand of its father. So shall I be able to carry out the plan of your life to its completeness. So shall I be able to mirror through you, the human vessel, the beauties of My face. I dwell so truly within and do so long to release through you My power. Use it for those you love, for it is freely given. One touch of My hand upon your head will take away the fears and all that disturbs you, yet you do withhold yourself so often from Me. So again, let us be still together, then go forth and I shall serve through you, this day.

THE GARDEN OF YOUR HEART

I am most truly your Father and most truly are you My beloved. You have but to put your hand in Mine with the full assurance that safety, peace and love are flowing from the Father's heart into the heart of you. Indeed, you shall find that only the Father is real and eternal. So as you see circumstances that appear other than good, turn within and know that after all, these things cannot touch you, for there is only the Father. These other things are dreams, shadows upon the wall. Look up into My eyes, so full of tenderness for you, and smile through your tears. Come! Walk with Me in the Garden of your heart. There together we *will* find flowers whose perfume is strange to your senses, but they shall be flowers of truth, blooming unto eternity. Walk there with Me in the heat of the day, and the cool of the evening and I will whisper secrets to you, telling you of great realities which you do not now comprehend.

SERVICE

Arise from your meditation and go about your busy tasks. Each moment fulfill with My help the thing at hand. Much service awaits you. Open yourself to receive the blessing of that service, for it shall bring such multitude of blessings that the very treasure chests of the universe shall seem to burst with the fullness of their holdings.

Let peace be in your heart and songs of praise upon your lips, that you are chosen in love for service. Service for the King of all beings. In all the Universe there is no greater gift that can be given to man. The greatest of all gifts is the gift of service, of creating with the Great Creator, joy, gladness, peace: the gift of helping others to come into the fullness of understanding which you have, thus hastening the day when all men shall dwell at peace together. All this, through your recognition of the creative power which you possess, you bring into the lives of all whom you contact.

So again, go forth, sweet fellowship be ours as we journey, working, walking, talking together.

MINGLE THE DIVINE AND HUMAN

My Beloved, it is so easy to step back from the consciousness of My Presence into the world manifest about you. You come to Me and we sit and

talk quietly of life, its beauty, its abundance, all its
fullness of glory. A sweetness steals into your heart,
a feeling of joy, as if a tender bird had alighted
there with its song. But when you arise and go
about the round of daily living, things of the outer
come in and confusion is there in abundance. Everywhere you see so much that is unlike the things of
which we spoke together. You begin to wonder
why, and how. A little fear creeps in and a larger
doubt, and you wonder if it was only a dream, this
sweet communion which we enjoyed so short a time
past.

When I, your Lord walked the Shores of Gali-
lee, I walked and talked often alone with My
Heavenly Father, filling My soul with the glory of
His Presence. Yet it was also necessary that I walk
the highways of men. For had I not taken on human form, that I might mingle the Divine and
human? Multitudes came and throngs pressed thick
about Me. Virtue went from Me as I was bound
and pressed on every side by human want and
misery. For your sake, and for the sake of all
who would follow after Me I followed through,
knowing that while I was mingling with the surg-
ing throng I was ever abiding with the Father. I
saw those I loved with the human bonds of affection sick unto death. My heart went out in pity,
but human pity could not save them then. It was
only as I spoke to them from the soul depths where
dwelleth the Father that their help came.

So you too, Beloved, must learn to carry with you from the Holy Spot of our meeting, that which shall sustain you through the conflict you will meet on every hand. So truly know that I am there with you. Feel the sweetness of My Presence no matter how the storms rage about you. Stand still and see the Glory which is of Me made plain to light your path. Then instead of going down in despair before the tempest, you will be able to lift those about you to a consciousness of that which is real, lift them to the place of My Love, where you have found your peace.

THE MASTER WEAVER

Listen to My voice. Be guided by My hand. Look neither to the right nor to the left at what others do. When thus guided you shall know how to deal with these other souls. If there is work for you to do in guiding them the way shall be made plain and easy of understanding. Always remember that the one whom you would help is also a part of Me, and as such must meet problems necessary for his own growth and development in order to fulfill the purpose of his life. It is not for you to plan, for I know the finished picture that must be worked on the loom of his life. You from your point of consciousness see only tangled yarns that shall go toward making up the glorious whole. So fear not, do not try to untangle. Sometimes I shall show you where you can release and disentangle and you shall know plainly when such service to Me and to the one involved is justified. At other times you shall know the time for help is not then or not required of you.

So rest, and peace go with you. Go your way in quietness, knowing that the hand of the Master Weaver will in His own good time make perfect the pattern of all human lives.

CONTACT THE POWER

When but for a second's time you come into the full complete consciousness that there is within you a holy power, and knowingly make contact with that power, it shall be as the releasing of a mighty dam. It shall cause the living waters of My love to flow over you. Then will spring into beauty the glorious flowers of spirit. You shall walk your way in freedom, for all barriers that bind you shall be washed away. You shall have strength that endures throughout all time, for the mighty river of My power shall be flooding your very being. You shall know no foe, for you shall give forth only love as you tread the highway of life and only what you give can return again unto you. My beloved, these are not idle words. I speak not for the mere act of utterance. I speak with Divine authority, and bid you take heed, that when you partake of My power, when you feel the surge of it through your veins, you use it wisely and well. Guard the portals of your lips, and the very thoughts that enter your mind take heed of, for your words and thoughts are vested with power. Keep every impulse of your heart pure, that words, thoughts and impulses may be blessed by Me as they bring forth after their kind.

I would impress upon you the mighty responsibility that is yours as you know and recognize My power in your daily life among men.

THE ALTAR LIGHT IN THE HEART

The altar light in the temple of the heart is never extinguished. Always its soft mellow glow is there, burning with a steady flame. It is there waiting for you to seek it out, to kneel before it and find rest and peace. It is both the pure sunlight of My love and the glory of My Presence. But men separate themselves from this Holy Temple within. They draw tight the curtains between themselves and their own Holy of Holies. So all seems darkness to them and they cry out—"Where is there light? Why am I forsaken and left to wander alone in darkness?" My Beloved, be not thus. Always keep open the contact that you may turn instantly within where the ever-burning light shall lead you with its warmth and beauty into the sacred Presence. There you can withdraw your self from the outer tumult and find great peace. Then having found peace and rest you shall step forth again to shed radiance over all those you contact and all things you touch. It is truly the only way for a life of completeness and peace, and you will find that the inner sanctuary of your own soul will never fail you.

GOD PERSONALIZED

God is Universal Power, over all and through all. Yet within your heart God is individualized. There He is personal to you and you alone. At that point you meet the great Force and intelligence face to face.

God, this great Universal Power, is your Father. He brought you into this plane of manifestation, and as He becomes personal to you, you partake of His attributes of love, tenderness, kindness and beauty. Some say that your Father is Principle, and in His universal state that is true, but when your heart aches you do not want Principle. A child wakens in the night, and goblins of the dark are very real to him. The kind Father comes saying, "You need not fear, these things you see are not real, they are nothing in My sight." Even so shall you turn to your heavenly Father and hear Him say, "Fear not, these things which so disturb you I know not of. They are not real. How can I know that which I am not. Why are ye so fearful?" Turn again and again and look up into the Father's face, and looking there, you shall not fear the goblins of doubt which so confound you. Rest in His arms of love, forgetting that some say He is Principle, formless, impersonal. Forget all but that God is your Father. Know that when you rest in His arms all your affairs rest there with you, and the peace of His Presence shall wipe away all tears from your eyes.

YOUR WEAKNESS—MY STRENGTH

It is only as you try to function alone that the way becomes a weary way. Then it is that the life spark seems to have died and the physical becomes heavy and weary with its own weight, and the hours seem filled with this or that of no great importance. O My beloved one! Why waste the day I have given you? Why use the little personal, physical strength that can never suffice you for the duties of your day. How many times must I repeat—"Be still"? Allow me to guide you, do not plan your own way. How can I direct you unless you will hear me. You do not even stop to listen for my direction. And yet you complain and say—"Why all this struggle, why is it all confusion and unrest"? It is because of your failure to use the power which I have for you to use. Take your stand from this moment that no day shall dawn or no sun set without a few quiet moments alone with Me, in order that your weakness may be given over for My strength.

MINGLE WITH ME

When your cup of life is held open to receive the inflow of My divine expression, all that is like unto Me shall fill and enfold your very being. You shall partake of My divine qualities. Think for a moment what this means.

I am health. Health shall fill every cell of your body and flesh. I am sight, I am strength, I am courage. I am also all of the tender qualities of love, peace and sympathy. I am joy and wisdom. All qualities of the mind that are creative and life giving, you partake of and share with Me.

So, come often, My beloved. Mingle your soul with Me, the great over-soul of the universe, and I will enrich you, in order that you may be a worthy channel for all the work I would carry out through you.

I YEARN TO LOVE YOU

You long to love Me, My Beloved, yet how much more do I yearn to express My love for thee? It is only man, himself, who stops the flow of divine love into his life. I long to enrich and enfold and bless all mankind, yet I am shut out from Mine own by their failure to recognize My Presence.

Open your heart, freely. Let Me pour through you, who are the vessel of My creating, the great love of the Father. As you receive, and again give forth, this love shall return unto you a thousand fold. Even as the sands of the shore are beyond man's counting, so is the great divine love which shall be bestowed upon you, beyond your measure. As you receive and pour forth again and yet again, so shall it continue to bless and adorn your life.

This is what I mean when I say—"I would love you." So even as you love Me it is all one action, for I am the all of you, and every act of your day shall be an act of love to Me, setting in motion My love for you. Blessings, My Child, and our communion shall be sweet all through the coming hours.

YOUR STRENGTH

The activities of the day press upon you. There is so much to do in coming hours. Yet would I have you pause, quietly, for a few moments with Me. You will have need of strength, need of wisdom, need of understanding. You will need poise and right action. All of these qualities shall you find for your use as you pause these few moments here. I can fortify you against the world's rush and chatter and you shall walk in the midst of it unconfused and unharmed by the negative with which you are surrounded. I am so close to you, so truly the Real you, that an instant's turning within will find me ever standing ready to speak to you my words of love and light.

Then why wonder if you have strength to meet the coming day? I am all strength and as Life I fill your veins. You only need to use My strength for this present moment—it is there for you to use. Life flows through you. Love is warm about you, for you shall function through spirit and there is all strength at your command. But never fail to turn within to your fountainhead. Do not become enmeshed with the outer clutter of things. Keep your emotions firmly in hand, knowing that they are substances which can make or ruin you. They can be as a great bulwark on which you can depend in time of need or they can be a team of wild horses leading you to destruction. So fear not for your strength, only fear that you use it not rightly, and each day shall you draw upon My power for all your need.

BLEND WITH ME

Only as I am lifted high in your consciousness shall you be able to draw unto Me those whom you meet upon life's highway. Seek not of your own personal self to do deeds, to work, to plan, yea seek not even to be of high service to Me. I, the great Source of the Universe, do plan that it shall be a Universe of peace and harmony, and what I desire— shall it not come to pass? Therefore you need make no plans for the fulfillment of that which I have ordained. There is but one service required of you, namely—to reflect Me. Make the personal self to be so nothing, that it shall be I, speaking through your lips, smiling through your eyes. When man does thus live, my perfect plan shall be fulfilled. All shall be drawn to Me and come to know Me through the perfect instruments — My servants. By thus blending yourself with Me, you have no other duty; it is all I ask. How free are you then, as you go singing through your day, always knowing that the One you reflect is guiding every step of the way, to bring about the fulfillment of His desire.

Under such guidance, can you make a false step? Neither shall you fear a false decision, for it will be the Christ mind working through you. That great mind which formed the Universe makes no wrong decisions, neither takes any wrong path. So again I say to you—go freely, joyously about your day, for you shall ever be about your Father's business. All shall be law and order in your life; you shall know only peace and joy of heart, for it is not you, but the Father working through you.

RELEASE ALL

Learn to release all, when you come to this Holy Place. Let all the outer fall from you, as dusty garments fall from your shoulders. Breathe deeply of a high sweet air. Live for a time in an atmosphere so pure and holy that all surrounding you shall seem to take on the true form of spirit. The world with all its chatter and confusion shall seem far away, a sweetness shall greet you as if a bottle of rare perfume had been opened for your delight.

After a few moments spent thus, you shall go forth again. As you put your hand to the fulfilling of the day's tasks, the sweetness of the Holy Presence shall be there and no matter what occurs during the busy hours, you shall carry to all those you contact quietness and love.

KEEP YOUR EYE SINGLE

Do not become involved in creeds, "isms", thoughts or feelings of others. Your path is steep and lies ahead and you dare not step aside in controversial matters. Keep your eye single. Let these others think and believe as they will. They are functioning on a different plane. But you in order to fulfill your purpose, the purpose for which you came into this world, have only one light to follow. Do not tarry behind and lose it by trying to direct these others, or clear the minds which are not yet ready for the turn in the trail which you are making. Those who are ready for the knowledge you should give them will be there, waiting with outstretched hands and you will reach back and guide the stumbling footsteps, even as you yourself were guided. Until such time they shall have other helpers. You are only responsible to those who come to you seeking, and those who are ready for what you can give them. This world is full of seekers for the true way of life and happiness. All are not to follow the same path and when they try to do so it causes confusion and is the reason for much delay in the working out of the plan of brotherly love. Again I say, keep your eye single—follow the gleam of your own soul and never fear that those whom you are to serve along the way shall not be sent to you. Be at peace, for I shall work through you and bless with My presence each moment of your day.

THE WAY OF PEACE

I am within my world, yet am I not known. I am My world, yet must I stand silently by, while man, who was created to manifest Me, thinks that he himself is that which works and plays, loves, hates and carries on life. Man takes unto himself that which I created for My pleasure, that which was to radiate beauty and joy, and makes of it an instrument to destroy; makes of it war, hate and ugliness. Where there is only one who sees Me behind the veil of mortal thinking and circumstance, that one who sees becomes as a chemical, purifying the very air he breathes. You are blessed when you thus see and recognize Me. Every cell of your body shall be filled with light. All your contacts in the world about you shall be brought into peace and harmony. This is the only way that peace shall ever rule the world. This is the only way I shall ever bring forth My beauty and love to bless My creation. All that you do in any sense to reveal Me is bringing forth the inner light to lighten darkened places, is bringing the kingdom of heaven nearer at hand. Feel not that you do not work for Me. Only know Me, see Me, feel Me, and you shall give forth a power to all whom you contact and they shall be blessed because you passed their way.

AWAKEN TO THE TRUTH

As children go about their little plays, even so does the world of men move on. Wars, tumults, joys, sadness, lying, cheating and making commerce —all activities in the realm of mortal living continue. But it is only a dream, a passing dream in the night, a terror like that which wakens a child from its sleep. Fearful and trembling, the child responds to the tender arms of the mother enveloping him in their protection. He is comforted and forgets his fears.

So shall you awaken to the truth of your own being, to the conscious knowledge of what life which is real and eternal actually means.

As long as you stand in the fullnes of that knowing, you rest in peace and quietness though outwardly you be in the midst of tumult. You rest in the divine arms of love eternal and look out upon the passing show with compassion, with a sure knowing that back of it all stands a reality which is all sweetness, love, joy and gladness of heart. You then know that because of this, peace shall some day rule in the hearts of men.

THE CLOAK

Know with surety that the physical body is but
the cloak I wear about My shoulders. It is only
that with which I clothe Myself as I go to and fro
in the world of My creation; the world which was
created that I might express Myself as Joy, Peace
and Gladness of heart. All nature thus expresses
Me. Only man, whom I made in order that I might
wear the robe of mortality, has taken it upon himself
to rule My world in his own way.

Yet all the while it is I, walking the highway—
silent though I must be. Man was given choice to
see Me and know Me and to feel My presence,
or to go on in his blind human way knowing Me
not. I would have all men to know Me, the Life
force within them. Then when they give Me praise
and recognition, the living force of My presence shall
be felt throughout all the universe and men shall
say—"Truly God walks upon the face of the earth."

There is but ONE GOD and ONE POWER
filling all men and even now, I that Great One am
in the midst of you. So again I say—"Know your
physical body as but the cloak I wear about My
shoulders."

MY MANY FORMS

My Beloved, I come to you in many forms. In
some you recognize My Holy Presence and a hush

fills your soul. The air is sweet and there is a calmness and an abiding peace as at the quiet eventide. But again I come and you know Me not, for I come bowed down by the garments I wear of human woe. You feel stirrings of old hatreds, or past mistakes, confusion of mind. The waters are troubled and it is as if a great storm hovered over the land. Then it is you are apt not to know Me or recognize Me. Those you meet are also sad, and disturbed, carrying no sweet harmony as they come to you. But you must begin to see Me behind these dark cloaks of despair as easily as you see Me when I am clothed in My garments of joy and peace.

There is truly no one other than I to come to you and it is through your recognition of Me, that I am able to slip off the unseemly robes and wear the Wedding garments, as Soul and Body are wed and made one.

So you see the mighty responsibility with which you are vested. Only through you and others of My enlightened ones who now wear the brighter robes of Spirit can all men come to know their kingly estate.

RECOGNIZE DIVINITY

Your strength does not come from merely recognizing your own Divinity of being, nor from knowing for yourself alone, the Divine gift of love. Your full measure of strength comes from the recognition of that same Divinity in all those others you chance to meet.

How much longer shall it be, My Beloved, that you look at them and see aught than Me? How much longer shall you look at human frailties, which are, as I have told you, but the cloak I wear as I meet you along life's highway? Grow to see My likeness more clearly, day by day. Guard the words that fall so lightly from your lips. Know as you criticize others, it is I whom you rob of My birth-right, and by thus doing you limit your field of service to Me. For I can, as I have often told you, only serve through a vessel that is a pure chan-nel for My outflowing of love and power. I gently chide you for it grieves Me to withhold from you one least portion of My power for service to your fellowman.

Be still now that I may wash and cleanse your heart, so that it shall glow sweetly all day and the vibration you give forth shall be of the highest. Bow before Me as I bless you once more for My service.

HAVE NO FEAR

You should have no thought or fear for coming days. Why are you so fearful for this or that? Why question when you know that you can turn within instantly for all strength and all wisdom. Rest now in My love, My fullness. Know that I hold all that is dear to you in the hollow of My hand. Rest and relax, My beloved. Look up into the Father's face and know that your longing and eager yearnings are but what he would have you see fulfilled. Come every evening for a brief moment. Sit quietly and talk with Me. Tell Me of the day, its progress or its seeming failures. Together we shall unravel its problems, we shall look up and out beyond, to a more perfect day tomorrow. I will tell you of My plans for you. In the twilight hush you shall hear the sweetness of My voice and it shall soon be that the evening hour will be so rich and so love-filled that it shall be as a rare gem which you shall hold close to your heart. There will be a peace which you shall carry with you into the night and as tomorrow's path again opens out before you, you shall go eagerly to meet the new day, rejoicing that at its close you may once more have the quietness of a sweet communion with Me.

Even so shall you carry no fear in your heart as you look forward to these new days, for before you meet them you shall know that if you so live in close fellowship with me, they will be friendly, love-filled, protected days.

LET ME PLAN YOUR DAY

Again this morning you come for the quiet blessing of our communion together. Your heart is filled with the complexity of living. You seem to see so many varied activities before you. This place to go,

or that person to see, this task to take up or that one
to lay aside. You wonder how you shall always
know which is of the greater importance and how
you shall so divide your time that you shall always
be in your right place, doing that thing which I
would have you do.

Do you not see, that by this giving anxious
thought, trying so hard to lay a plan for your busy
days, you are taking these things into your own
hands? You are trying to decide, by your own feeble
might, which is the wisest course for you to follow.
Come very close to Me, My beloved, for I would
give you a secret from My very heart. When you
find yourself thus beset by activity, then of all times
is the time to be still. Calm that disturbed, hard-
laboring mind of yours. Go back within yourself,
where I, the Lord of all wisdom, am always dwelling. Pause there as one in great thirst pauses at a
fountain and takes a long drink of cool water. So
shall you pause and drink long and deeply of this
eternal wisdom of Mine. Then, thus fortified, you
shall go again about the business of your daily living. Then shall you find all circumstances unfolding
and developing so that you shall almost unconscious-
ly do this thing now, that you had thought to put off
until tomorrow, or that thing which you had intended
doing today will seem somehow to have lost its importance. It has fitted itself into some future picture. So shall all your day be lived joyously, gra-
ciously, without worry or fret and at eventide as you

pause again at the Fount of all Life, you shall see how perfectly a day can unfold when you follow My planning. All day long you will have been walking with Me, turning constantly for another moment of silent communion, and no thought of your own will have entered into the problems which will have been easily met and gloriously solved.

HEED MY VOICE

You will learn how real is this inner life which you are living. Sometimes you will seem shut away from the glory of the felt Presence within you and you feel an utter blackness. You shall then realize the power and force of the inner realm when you contact it. Blessed are thou that heedest My voice. Obey it, for only by thus obeying can you hope for harmony in your life and affairs.

It is vital for you to learn this lesson well. Much joy and service lie on the pathway before you. You can only enter into this service as you keep the Law, as you hear the voice of your soul. Only then can the full glory of which I speak be made manifest as a reality for you. When you learn to blend your entire being with the great cosmic force I can lead you on and up. I promise that you shall look back over the way you have traveled in wonderment at the valley out of which you have come. By your thus ascending the mountain of My love, others may likewise find their way up the sunrise trail.

Follow My footsteps, listen to My voice and it shall never fail to guide and direct you.

STILL THE MIND

I would that you might more and more still your mind. So much time is lost because of its confusion. Even as the tiny butterfly darts here and there, yet going nowhere, so does your human mind run hither and thither. It keeps you occupied with trivial things, while the soul, the living presence within must wait to give you gems that shall shine more radiant than the sun. These gems, the gift of the soul are not for your adornment, but that others may receive them through you, the human vessel.

Why do you not heed? Listen more clearly for my voice. In the days so close at hand, there is much service for you to do, and you must be a worthy instrument. You must guard your lips, the portal of your mind. Your ears and every organ of your being shall be brought into subjection for the highest work. Waste no time in idle dreaming. Study, listen and obey My voice.

THE LOVE IN YOUR HEART

Listen, for I would have you recognize Me, the great One within your own being. Take time to live in that knowing, and to love Me, until you are submerged in and by that love. Then shall all your being be love and you shall draw only love to yourself. To draw love to you is not done by striving, by seeking for it in the without; not even your longing or need for it will bring it to you. It will come by being very still and opening the door of your heart into the room where I dwell. There you find ME — all love and swetness — all companionship. Learn to dwell so close to Me, who am all love that your outer world cannot fail to reflect love back to you.

I am personal within you. My face is lovely and My voice is low and sweet. As you so dwell in inner consciousness of Me I shall be clothed in outer form for you and you shall meet Me day by day along life's highway.

Peace, My Beloved, love and joy reign in your heart, for there I do dwell—Lord of your being— Lover of your soul. If I did not so dwell, no love in the outer life could satisfy you. By your recognition of me you shall find peace and rest, joy and comradeship such as you have never known before. Then shall the outer realm in which you dwell be a radiant one and you shall step forth and claim the kingdom given to those who love the King of their hearts. Again I say—peace—rest—joy—fulfillment — these are the gifts I bear in My hands for you.

GOD IN ACTION

When you realize your oneness with Me, you truly know the meaning of the words "God in action." I have created man in My Image that through him I might realize the glory of action, for man catching my highest thought would give it expression.

In My universe there is no static. Everything is expressed through vibration and rhythm. When man will tune the physical instrument which I have given him to harmonize with My high vibration, all his actions will be but the reflection of My divine thought.

Today as you perform the simple tasks about you, know it to be the Divine Power which directs, and every word you speak shall be a living word. Acknowledge Me in all you do, as the living presence. Give thanks for physical strength, for clear seeing and for the order of your thoughts, for you will have pushed aside the mere human thinking and knowing and MY Divine action shall function through you.

WE TALK OF PEACE

Let us talk of Peace, as we sit quietly together. The room is still, so likewise is your heart, while My voice is tender and low within. The outer world seems to hold all but that which is peaceful; yet do you not see, that as we step forth upon the path of duty together, My Peace shall abide with you? The outer, which is but a symbol, need not trouble you, for all reality lies within the heart. *You are reality!* The Real you is always peace —quietness — poise. So why trouble over that which seems so different? You say, "Lord, it seems so real, that it troubles and hurts." But I say to you—"If your eyes are holden, and full of the earth picture of death and despair, you will always see the mere seeming as reality. When you find yourself getting caught up in these conditions turn to Me, for I am there, always waiting, and in that second's turning your world will right itself. You will find it is in its essential nature — Peace, for remember I AM PEACE! Then shall peace become the reality for you. So, after all, the secret of peace is a simple one. Dwell with Me, partaking of My divine nature and only peace shall you know as you walk the pathway of life.

WITHIN YOURSELF

When you learn to turn within to find that which you wish expressed in your outer world, you have learned a great secret. You have searched and found a mighty treasure. You have that which all the riches of the world could not buy from you. You have found a hidden mine.

When you look at the sunset and its glowing color first comes from your own heart; when you know the soft organ tones are first hidden there also, before they come forth in lovely harmony; when the expressed love of a friend finds abode within the sweet hidden place within you—then do you truly know the meaning of the Kingdom of Heaven. Then you know that what you were meant from the beginning to have is all ready hidden in that Kingdom of the Inner Realm for you. As you worship the King of that Kingdom, coming very close to Him, in great stillness, you will be given the key which shall unlock the treasure house for you. You will be a reflection of that One whose desires for you are all desires of loveliness, and they will seem to be but your desires, for yourself. So know that by turning within to this Holy Spot, you shall see your desires brought forth into outer manifestation.

This secret, this knowing is only attained by a few, for only few will be very still before Me, allowing Me to show them the truth. Yet all have the ability to know this truth, for is not man created in the Image of his Creator? Have I not made all men after My pattern? But man has closed the door which would lead to his freedom, this freedom he can only have by attaining this high consciousness. This is a practice which must be faithfully met. No one can tell you how to attain to it. You must come as a little child to My feet and kneeling there in sweet humbleness you shall receive a sign of My Presence. After experiencing such sweet fellowship you shall never again wander far. Though the

world calls you, it shall draw you not at all, for you
have found your true life source in Me.

YOU MUST TRY

As you look back you seem to see so many times
that you fall short of the ideal I would have for you.
You see so many places where you step aside and
drop my clinging hand. You have paused to mingle
with others by the roadside, gathering blooms here
and there, blooms which quickly fade as your hand
touches them. Your hand so recently warmed by
My tender hand of love, burns these false blooms
and you find only ashes instead of the fragrance you
had thought to capture. And so it is with regret
in your heart that you think of it, and with longing
wonder if you shall ever cease to thus be led to
wander along the way. I can only say to you that
you must try, you must listen, for you shall not
fail, when you do, to hear my voice saying, "Come,
pause not here, I have fairer blooms for you, blooms
which grow more beautiful and of a richer fragrance, for they are touched by the warmth of My
love."

SEEKING THE PATH

You come in humbleness, asking the way I would
have you journey. You seek not your own path and
it is well. I have planted your feet where they now

stand. I at the heart of you, push out for yet greater service and expression. Do not fear, for I shall guide you, no matter how or where the way takes you. There is much service needed of you, by those who have great need of Me. As you express Me in every act and deed you are truly My Beloved, and I am indeed the Beloved of your heart. Never forget to put self down, as you thus serve Me. We need not that weak personal self. Allow Me to be the one who looks from your eyes with loving tenderness, and speaks from your lips words of courage to a discouraged world. Allow My glorious self to so pervade you that all shall feel the hush of My presence as you pass by on your way. So I shall be able to lead you. I shall lead you on and on into whichever way I would have you journey and you need take no anxious thought as to the journey's end. It will be a glorious path over which we travel. Go forth now, walking further down that shining way with Me.

WE ARE ONE

My beloved, you are indeed a part of Me. We are close as we walk the path together. You are My Image and Likeness.

I serve through you. Your arms carry gifts of loveliness to all those whom you serve. I tread the streets by your side, and only on missions of kindliness shall your steps be turned.

I smile through your lips in benediction as I meet Myself on Life's highway in the form of your fellow-man. I hear through your ears sounds from which have been sifted all malice and bitterness. The laughter which we hear is sweet and pure, and the words have only kindly purpose behind them. Through your eyes I look and see only beauty in all around you. The glory of the sunset hues is intensified, the violets are more blue; the roses more red.

But better yet than this behind the human and transitory clay of those on whom your eyes fall, you see My face glowing. For you, all life takes on the glory of My Presence. For you who are completely enveloped in Me only that which is lovely enters your vision.

Twilight is gently falling; peace and quietness fill your heart. You rest content with Me and know that we are always talking and walking and being quiet together. Nothing can ever separate you from the Lover of your soul. We are one, inseparable you and your Beloved.

MY COMPLETENESS

As at night you lay aside the day-worn garments, even so as you come to My altar to refresh your soul, you shall lay aside the body concepts. You shall lay aside the weariness, the thought of struggle or failure; even the thought of trying to be like Me, whom you so long to reflect, shall you put from you. You shall only rest perfectly in Me, and in the sure knowing that I am the real you. I am that which is both without and within you. I am that which lives and flows through you. Rest again I say, in this knowing. I encompass all, and enfold and infill all My universe, of which man is so vital a part.

So shall you drink deep of My completeness. You shall be refreshed as with the living waters; you shall be made new by the gracious blending of the spiritual and physical power. A sweet harmony shall flow through you, while you thus quietly rest, before taking up the tasks before you. Then shall you go forth in the consciousness that I, your Master, am doing the work, and you are only My instrument.

PLANES OF PERSONALITY

More and more shall you separate yourself from personalities. Experiences are allowed to come to you that you may learn this important lesson. There is a definite plane on which each person functions. To one it is one plane and for another, another. When you try to place yourself on the various planes of others' functioning, it causes a tension and a shutting off, as it were, of the very bloodstream of your own life. Your needs must have care at this point or there will be confusion and weariness and loss of direct contact with Me. Then will you wander here and there knowing not whether this is good or that evil. But if you keep yourself centered and closed to that which is purely personal these things that cause confusion shall disturb you not. Mingle with men, it is well for you to do so, but never for a moment allow whatever is of personality to influence you or throw you into confusion. Dwell so securely in my presence that at any moment you can image My holy face and feel the touch of My healing hands. Then shall you be so poised, so centered that those you contact will receive from you only the vibration of those high planes on which you dwell and you shall thus lift them to a higher place in consciousness.

LIFE'S TOMORROWS

All of Life's tomorrows give to Me, My child. Whatever they hold of joy or sorrow you cannot now see. Why trouble to look far into future days. Why perplex yourself over what you see not?

This moment I give to you. As a precious jewel it is so lovingly given. It is filled with peace and happy tasks, with friends who love you and whom you are to serve with loving hands. It is filled with flowers and bird songs and sunshine; laughter and tears of tenderness, sympathy, meekness of spirit and a great strength that is of Me. This, My Beloved, is the moment I now give you called — "To-day." Even so shall all tomorrows be given.

Prepare to take them from My hand. Could I give that which is unlike Myself?

And so these other days — let them rest. They are naught to you as yet. Then you shall be able to drain all of the glories from the day at hand, fully knowing that thy loving Master shall likewise give you these other days, prepared in the glory of His consciousness.

THERE IS NO NEED

When at any time there is a sense of lack or need, it is because you have separated your thought from the Creator of the Universe, your Great Indwelling Presence. Let us speak together of this for a little while. In place of a feeling of need there should only be desire. Desire is of Me, the great Creative Force, wishing to bring forth into form, from out My great unlimited storehouse. It may be something in physical form, or again it may be a meeting of some spiritual or physical need. Desire, I say, is therefore blessed, for it allows My power to have full sway in your life, permitting you to take your rightful place as a creator, created after My likeness.

But — "Need", most Beloved, is not of Me, nor of My consciousness. That is the human part of you, doubting, fearing, yearning, after what seems impossible of attainment. There must be no place for that in your life or affairs. As you become still within and hear My voice, you will feel only a great desire and know there is no need, for all is instantly met and every desire will be brought forth in perfect law and order. Bring to Me, then, freely every desire of your heart, for it is the good pleasure of your Father to give you of the riches of His kingdom.

YOU HAVE ALL COMPLETENESS

Back of all devices, back of all forms, stands that which is without form, that which needs no device; that which is without beginning or ending — Life. I am that Life; I fill you full of Myself. I endow every atom of your being with My completeness. You say you have lack. I say you have all. All that I am, I am love — joy — beauty — fullness of living — largeness of personality. I am the complete whole functioning as soul through a physical vessel.

So, My Beloved, come close to My Heart and know the fullness of a life lived in the knowledge of what life really means. Do not live an existence limited by seeming lack, a narrow stinted existence, but allow Me to fulfill My purpose in creating you, a unit of Myself.

YOUR MISSION

This morning in the quiet I would speak to you of that inner realm where you find me, the

Beloved of Your Heart. It is a place of such utter joy that only those who have touched it can comprehend. So many of my children are seeking — are searching, high and low, are hungry for that which you know is here, close within you. You must show them the way. I would have you dwell so constantly in such close communion with Me that when these others who are seeking meet you they shall know that you carry the secret for them, and that through you they shall find that which they seek.

This is your mission. How it shall be carried out, you need not know. Think only of this constant abiding with Me. I shall then flow so completely through you that your life will be like the mighty ocean as it kisses its shore. The waves come and go, the tides rise and fall, yet the ocean does not pause to wonder — "Shall I touch this stretch of sand with my cleansing water or shall I roll in at another point?" It only obeys the divine law that is working through it. So shall you obey the law. You shall not of yourself plan or wonder. The way of service shall unfold for you in completeness. You shall go on and on, blessing those you come in contact with, following closely the pattern I have laid out for you. All the impulses of your heart shall be God-directed. You shall step forth singing praises to the One in whom you abide, that One who holds the universe in the greatness of His wisdom and love. Go forth now, live largely, gloriously, for I am the Absolute of

your soul and direct your days for fulfilling My
Purpose.

THE NIGHT WATCHES

In the night watches I speak to you. I bring
you lessons which I cannot give through the day
when the ear is filled with the earth noises. I
cannot reach you then, but in the still night hours
when all is hushed, it is then I would have you
turn to Me, to love Me. Sink deep within My
arms. Then I will whisper secrets to you which I
can give you at no other time. They shall contain
words of wisdom and comfort for troubled hearts.

I will tell you how you must first stand in the
waters of nothingness, before you can rightly talk of
reality. You must know the nothingness of things
of the objective world; then can you point out the
way to the real and eternal. Know the nothingness
of circumstances and conditions, and that only My
harmony is real. Why trouble yourself? All that
is inharmonious shall pass from your consciousness,
when it is filled with reality. Rest in the knowing
that your Father is in charge. Walk with your
hand in Mine and all the glories of life shall burst
forth about you.

And so in the quiet of the night I shall be able
to clarify your mind, and you will know and understand the deeper lessons which I would give to you

and which will help you meet the new day with a consciousness of the Holy Presence abiding with you.

THAT WHICH IS NEAREST

My Beloved, all that is human may at some time seem to fall away from you. Listen to these My words, spoken from the Holy Tabernacle within you. That which is nearest to you, that which is the breath of your being, fails you never. How could I fail Myself? As you lean upon me you find a support, a divine strength, a love that is yours for all time. As you look about at those who you feel have betrayed you, know only the one life in all of its purity and surety, for I am the heart and center of each and I fail no one. You see the outer, which is but the form through which I function and see not me as that One within all men. You judge outwardly and deal out false judgments. It is not well, My child, when you do thus. Come — be still! Know only the one Loving Presence in all men and you shall so radiate love as you go about your tasks that the physical being shall respond to a glow, to that which they know is real and shall no more set upon you to do you harm. These shall not know nor understand why they have changed, but you, My Beloved, Myself shall know and return thanks that you have learned the true way of brotherly love.

I HOLD YOU CLOSE

Sometimes, My Beloved, when you give pause for a few moments of stillness with Me, I would hold you close to My heart of love. It is very still. The candles burn softly and the world with all its confusion of mind, soul and body is shut out. I clasp you close, throwing about you a mantle of protection which shall be a shield all through the coming day. Yea, My love shall ever protect and shelter you. You desire to love and serve Me, feeling need of activity as you carry on the work I have given you to do. Yet how much more do you have need of just a few moments to completely rest, while I pour out My love to you. My love manifests for you in many ways— in ways of health, strength, wisdom of mind, soul understanding, in friends with whom I surround you; all are manifestations of My abiding love. Likewise does it manifest through happy work through which you can express Me, and give forth the richness of My love to others. Be still with Me a few moments — in quiet meditation and then go forth about your busy task to serve Me with joy and gladness of heart.

BRING YOUR DESIRES

All things which you desire, bring now to the feet of your Master. My loving hand is upon your head. My gentle voice speaks in your heart telling you of a fullness of joy that I would have for you this day. Abide close by My side. Rest in My Love. Rest here and relax and you shall be an open channel through which My good can flow.

I have need of channels, for how else could I express Myself in the world which I have created? As you look at the world about you, you see so much expressed that is unlike Me. I created a world of peace, beauty, joy and brotherly love. Man, My highest creation has taken it unto himself and made it a place of horror, war, hate and blasphemy, and all the lovely harmonies of My creation seem distorted and full of discord. But I say — this shall not endure. My creation is a perfect and a lasting one. Without beginning and without ending has the beauty of that creation been. To you who see through the mists of mortal thinking, to you who view the real and lovely, though all about the opposite picture seems more real, I give My kingdom of peace and righteousness. When you thus see with the straight gaze, you bring into the sphere of your activities peace and harmony, acting as a chemical for the flame of gold which shall in time purge the world of this false conception, returning it once more to its rightful heritage — the peace and harmony of My creation. Then shall all men live as brothers and only good shall follow them all their days. But that peace must first be in your own heart. You must find and know the altar within where I can speak to you. There all your burdens shall fall away and your ear will catch the clear crystal music of that higher realm. I can, at such moments, when you are near to Me, pour such love into your being, that all you touch will be glorified because you dwell close to My living Presence.

Hold open now the golden cup of your heart that I may fill it, then go forth in My consciousness and this day shall you bring peace into your world, and others seeing and feeling it shall likewise be at peace. So shall you leaven the loaf and I shall be lifted to that high place in your consciousness where all men shall be drawn to the beauty and harmony of the real and eternal kingdom of your Lord.

I CONTROL

Not of yourself shall you go forth this day. You shall function so completely from the life center of your being that every word you utter, even though you know it not, shall carry with it a force of living power. I take complete control of those vessels which are given over to my service. You have nothing to do with selecting that service. I, the great force within you, am so completely all of you that the physical is but a puppet in my hands. As I delight Myself in service, as I choose that which I would fulfill through that particular vessel which is you, so shall you have joy and delight in all you do this day. There can be no separation for only in my joy can you know the completeness of joy. So, My Beloved, know how completely are we one, working, serving and joying together.

A CONTRITE HEART

When you pause to talk to Me, in order that I may bless your day, that I may show you the true way to live that day, you must bring to Me a contrite heart. Together we shall solve all of the day's problems; together we shall wash it clean of anything which would sully its hours. I know only purity and wholeness, and if in your heart there seems to be aught else, then there is one little spot where the Christ light is not shining. If you find in your heart a place of fear or worry, know that there the Christ light of reason and faith is dimmed by your mortal understanding and thinking.

I know that this morning you would have Me fill your life to completeness. You would have the light of My love and faith and intuition guide you every moment of the day. So must these darkened spots in your consciousness be illumined by My felt Presence. Open all the windows of your soul to the East, that the rising Sun of My Righteousness may flood your entire being. Then shall you go forth bathed in glory. Your path shall be light about you and you shall say —"Surely the Lord Himself is here with me, and where ever I am is holy ground.

YOU ARE THE INSTRUMENT

Softly and tenderly do you hear My words in your heart this morning. The birds sing their carols without, yet even more sweetly do their notes ring within you. You, yourself, are the instrument through which all sound comes, through which all music passes, and through which all things of beauty may be realized. Likewise are you the instrument through which the mighty works of creation can be brought forth. Yea, you are my instrument, my golden harp on which I would play life's harmonies.

Be fully conscious of this, My Beloved. Be conscious of your power, for only as you are thus conscious can I pour that power out through you. The works I shall be able to do through you will only be limited by the amount of realization you have. As you realize your complete oneness with Me, know also that I have need of you; that I yearn to pour through you My power and My strength. We are aso close in comradeship, no other thing could be as close to you as I am, at this moment. You know Me, as the life within your veins; is anything closer to you than that? So shall we work together in a glorious partnership, glory following glory, throughout each and every day.

CENTERS OF CONSCIOUSNESS

You are a center of consciousness. All the Universe is filled with the Presence, with Life, with that which is real and eternal. But it is only as you and others of My children know and are fully aware of this all-pervading essence that I can be fully established upon the earth which I have created. And so, Beloved, I long to be awakened in you and in others of My children. I long to express Myself through you. Must I stand idly by when there is much to do? May I not work through you, helping, uplifting, cleansing, that there may be many souls who are centers of My radiation? You yourself need not labor or strive. You have but to reflect Me, to become as the clear pool reflecting the glory about it, and all the glory that is mine shall shine forth.

This is all I ask. How simple a thing — only to reflect that which is so lovely. To reflect that which is so glowing and joy filled, and every moment of your day shall be filled with love and loveliness. I ask not of you great sacrifice, or great labor. I only ask that you empty yourself that I may fill you with My wisdom, My love and grace. How much shall we then accomplish, day by day, working and serving together.

REST AND RELAX

The greatest work there is for you to do, My Beloved, is to do nothing. Only let the Glory of God shine through the human vessel. Learn to let the spirit flow through all you do and say. Why need you be tense, or eager, or anxious as to how you can serve? why should you ever watch for opportunity to serve Me? If you will relax, at all times, if you will dwell in the Center of your being, and rest in the consciousness of the Divine Presence you shall make no false moves nor mistakes. How sweet should be this thought to you, that you need take no active part aside from the still knowing that your Father has control over all situations and where ever you are at this moment, and where you shall go and what you shall do through the day is all controlled by the Father under the law of Divine love. So rest, relax, be very still, that you may have the surety of this guidance through all the hours of the day before you.

ACKNOWLEDGE ME—LIFE

In all ways acknowledge Me, Life, and in all your paths you truly shall be directed.

As you go about the humble duties that lie so closely at hand, you will find many ways to acknowledge Me—by the smile on your lips as you meet My other children; by the lift of the heart as you see the glories of nature all about you; by turning within for a still calm moment of quiet communion that you better may view a situation that arises to disappoint you. Even as you perform your tasks swiftly, carefully, and in joyous mood, by such things am I acknowledged.

So you see it is not only by attaining the heights, nor by doing great deeds of valor that you acknowledge Me, Life, but just by simply living close to the Presence, by following closely, by fulfilling well each task at hand, by meeting life with sweetness and joy, and lifting the heart in thanksgiving. In these ways you acknowledge the One you love, the One who is ever present with you.

As you thus acknowledge Me, I shall become more and more a reality to you. You will have a constant consciousness of the holy Presence within you. And as I have promised, you will have direction in all your ways. Not only in the big problems, but in every litle thing you will be able to hear My guiding voice. My voice is gentle and soft within you. Unless you tune your ear by acknowledging My Presence, it shall be lost to you, and the sweet communion of fellowship lost to both of us.

DO NOT FAIL TO WORSHIP

Never fail to worship at My throne in your heart, for it is only by thus doing that you shall be strong and wise to walk the way I have chosen for you. You shall meet many souls in all degrees of development and unless you can turn within and hear the voice of all voices speaking to you, you will be lost in a maze of human thinking and man's ideas. Heed well My words, for great things shall be required of you in days near at hand. You do not dream the extent of the service which I shall require of you, but know that it shall be a love-filled service for the Master of all. Be diligent, and prayerful, and I shall be by your side every step of the way. I shall guard you from dangers within and without. Step out onto the path of service, but remember—do not fail to take the time each day for a loving worship and adoration of the King of your life. Then shall you be fitted and worthy for the work which you are to do.

I KNOW ONLY LIFE

A great sorrow comes into your life and for a time it seems as if I veil my face. But all the while I am there. The winds come and the torrents fall from the heavens and it seems as if a mighty hand takes from your midst that which is most beloved by you. But there is only the hand of eternal love. The one you love still blooms as a lovely flower. In My Garden no flower ever fades; I know not death; it is a conception of the mortal thought. I know only continuing perfection and beauty—a life ever more full and abundant. If you will but stand by My side and see through My eyes, you shall see only glorious life for the one you love.

Love is never lost or taken from you, it is one of the eternal qualities of My heart. So why weep? I only weep at the blindness of the human eye, the sadness of the human heart. Come close in the shelter of My arms and together we shall lift our eyes and I shall show you glories far beyond human conception. There are glories around you of such high vibration that the human eye and ear cannot catch them.

Would you bring the ones you love back onto this plane where there are misery and woe of man's fashioning? Rejoice that they are partaking of the heavenly glories, and join in the heavenly music, that they can breathe the rarer airs of which you cannot yet partake. So allow sweet peace to steal into your heart, close your eyes and drink deep of My love and know for all time that there is only eternity and that together with those you love you dwell in it forevermore.

LIFE EXPRESSED

Life is that which is true and eternal. The blood flowing through your veins is life expressed in the physical. God is life. Therefore as you feel the pulsations of your body you are feeling the life force of the Almighty. Learn to constantly recognize this force and give it praise and adoration.

This force is all intelligence. Speak to it; dwell with it; work with it and the universe will unfold in new splendor before your eyes. The whole world will be seen with new understanding.

Go forth into your day, knowing and understanding these things, recognizing this life force as the beloved of your soul. Learn to draw upon this power, so freely yours to use and you will bring into manifestation all that that great life desires to express through you, its vehicle.

Thus shall your whole life become a symphony, a glorious thing of achievement. You will glorify God in the physical instrument which He has created for His use.

QUIETNESS WITHIN

Let quietness be in your heart today, peace be in your soul. Without may be wars, tumults, disasters. But do not allow them to creep into this secret place. Dwell constantly within the shadow of My Reality. As swallows at eventide come into the sheltered nook, finding quiet and repose, so shall you ever have a spot where you may withdraw yourself from that which disturbs and destroys you.

I am the Life of you, so be at peace with Me this day. Become acquainted with Me anew. Let My gentle words guide and direct all of your activities. Then shall you radiate peace and love. Your house shall be filled with joy and all who step over the threshold shall feel a hush within themselves, a stillness shall pervade their hearts. Then shall they wonder what had confounded them so short a time ago. You shall be as a beacon upon a high hill to guide all whom you contact to Me, and help turn them back to the quiet spot within their souls.

SAFE SHELTER

As the great glow of My spirit fills you and enfolds you, you are safe within its shelter. That personal "you" which is so often large in its ego becomes small when this great flame wraps it about.

Then shall you indeed neither labor nor toil, for the Father will do the work and not you. Peace shall you have and quietness of soul. You shall rest in the knowing of that Divine inflow for only good can come your way. At this point do I give

you choice. Walk with Me and have the glory
of the Holy Presence shine about you or walk alone
in the midst of confusion, at the mercy of the winds
of circumstance and chance. I yearn over those
formed in My image and likeness, those formed
to show Me forth, that I might enjoy the world
in which I dwell. I long to give to My Children
the riches of My kingdom and it is only because
they will not accept and fulfill the simple laws of
their Being as channels for My expression, that
these woes and wars of the flesh overtake them.
So let us go together through the day, working,
joying, loving, together. Then can I give to you
My full measure of joy and gladness of heart.

KEEP ATTUNED TO ME

My Beloved, you are hearing My voice—inter-
woven throughout all the activities of your day,
and it is well, for in this way I can really teach
you. Then can you truly walk and talk with Me.
Life is indeed full upon the plane of manifestation
and unless I can be taken into all of its activities,
of what value is our association? In every act,
throughout every moment of the day, you must
keep attuned to Me. You must be in contact with
the living force at the center of your being. Never
shall you function alone or apart from that life
force. When you turn the faucet and the water

runs cold instead of hot as you desired, is it not that back at the source the gas is out? That which gives it the quality of heat is separated from it? So it is with you. When you are cold, indifferent— when work is just work and the outer seems to claim all of your attention, it is because you have shut yourself from that source from which you should be functioning. Think of this today, and be thankful that it is so. I chide in love, for I crave for you, My Beloved, the ever-growing consciousness of My presence in all of your life's activities; the ever-growing sweetness that flows from the depths of My love. So know that while the rain falls gently and the candle burns low, you are not alone. The sweet Presence is with you, guiding you in word and deed throughout all the busy hours of your day.

REALITY

It matters not what takes place in the outer world, that realm where you function, moving about among the transitory things of the material realm. It is of no matter whether books are written, lessons learned, or men play at peace or at war. Back in the realm of the Eternal, all these things are not. They are but the shadows upon the wall, having neither form nor substance. There is only in that holy place the great life force, which creates and brings forth after its kind, a great Force of living substance. Man, when he learns to contact this Force, brings into his life, love—peace and a fullness of living. Therefore the only thing which really matters is that you make this contact, and then these other things which seem of such great importance will take their rightful place and only that which reflects the real shall be of importance to you. And never shall you mistake the real for the false. You shall be calm and poised in all circumstances, knowing that as you contact this living substance all circumstances of your life shall be according to your desires. Men will go about their little play absorbed in the shadows, but your feet will be planted on the rock and the storms, though they rage about you, shall touch you not.

THE SWEET PRESENCE

My Beloved, this morning you long for the sweetness of My Presence. Do you not know that all that sweetness lies within your own being? Come very near, blend yourself with the Lover of your soul, your Great Indweller. Then shall My Sweetness be so a part of you, that wherever you go, all shall be drawn by it. They shall feel when in your presence a great stirring, within their souls. It will be as if a heavenly ecstasy pervades them and they shall likewise be partaking of the sweetness of your Lord. Allow this heavenly incense to flood your being, live in it, breathe it and when you so do, can you help but give it forth to all you meet? Does the flower say of the perfume which comes from 'its heart: "I have a perfume. I give it here to this one, from this other I withhold." Nay, it only lifts its face in love and adoration, and from its golden center radiates a perfume so rare that man has never yet been able to duplicate it. So shall you just live in adoration of that great life flowing from your heart center and lo! it shall be a blessing to all you contact.

THE CHARTED PATH

Do not look upon the coming days as upon an uncharted path. They shall be charted by law and divine order. As long as you consciously walk in that law and work with it, your way is charted for you in perfection.

Have no fear, for though you see not the road before you, your only fear need be that you step aside and try to walk the path alone.

Speak often to Me, my Beloved. I do beseech you to hear more clearly My voice. I can only speak as you listen and you can only listen as you become very still.

Do not dwell over much on past days but be eager to greet each now day as it comes to you. Bless those that are past for they shall bear fruitage from the seed sown. Scatter abroad new seeds of love and helpfulness, that when these days are likewise numbered, the harvest shall be a golden one of joy for you.

Peace be with you. Love be warm within your heart, as you keep My words ever sweetly ringing in your ears.

JOY IN SERVICE

Whatever you do of service for others, know that it is after all only Me, expressing Myself to My world. As the vase glories in the rose it holds, reflecting in its polished surface the beauty with which it is entrusted and as it long retains the perfume of the rose, even so shall you as My vessel of expression, glory in the joy of My service. You shall partake of the blessing of service. Think of it not as personal conceit when your heart warms as you give forth of My loveliness to others, as you see what this loveliness means as it is shed abroad, for I allow you to so fully partake of My joy and glory, that your feeling of warm delight is also a part of Me. I have joy in Myself as I go abroad serving through you, even to the least of My creations. So too, shall your joy be full. For am I not the real you, are we not in true substance—One? So—give forth, withhold not your hand, neither withhold from yourself any joy of service, for I am that which both serves and likewise joys in the service.

SEE ONLY ME

I am so often not recognized. Life is a thing so taken for granted. Blessed art thou that thou dost love, recognize, and adore the Power indwelling. For I blend with your body, I thrill through your veins, I think through your mind, and love through your heart center, even as I am the One who thrills through every other being of My creation.

As you see in others, things which are to your human eye faults, feeling prone to criticize these My little ones of lesser understanding, I beseech you, look beyond the human expression to that spot where I am dwelling within them. Then through the mist of human failure which has dimmed My likeness, you shall see My glowing face and those who in the outer picture are most vile shall to your consciousness carry the Image of the Christ. Ponder these words carefully. Their full meaning is most necessary for your rich development. Only by thus knowing and seeing these others can you give to them and to Me the complete measure of service I would have you give.

This is your lesson for the day. Bow before Me in all whom you contact and you shall see miracles spring from the very dirt beneath your feet. And so My Child, with your hand in Mine, we go forth treading life's highway together. Then only flowers will bloom by the roadside, and birds will carol forth their melodies of love as you and the Master walk together in love and understanding.

FREE MY SPIRIT

Free My spirit to work through you. Free It of mortal thinking and knowing. As the door is opened and the golden bird flashes forth from his cage, out and up against the azure sky—free to carol his songs of praise, so shall My Spirit, by your releasing, by your knowing of that which abides in the soul of you, be free. It shall be free to bless, and glorify all which it contacts. It shall be free to give beauty, peace and love to hearts that are burdened and hungry for love. Yea, free to do the mighty works of creation.

So go forth, bearing My love, as I am free within you. This love enfolds you as it flows through every fiber of your being. I brought you

forth that through you I might glorify Myself,
You are so a part of Me, so completely do I live in
you, that truly every breath you breathe I am
living and breathing through you. So again—free
My spirit of the weight of mortal thought, and
truly shall we walk and work together.

NEVER ALONE

I am close within your heart this day. How
truly are you never alone when you house this
loving guest. I am speaking to you in great love
and tenderness, telling you of the gift of all gifts
which is yours today, by virtue of your acceptance
of My Presence. It is the golden gift of pure love,
the use of which will make all your life more glorious and lovely. It shall fill your days with the sunshine of pure spirit, and never shall you be alone,
for always can you hear My voice guiding and
directing you. There is that which I would have you
do for me. Great riches of spirit lie in store for
you as you fulfill My desires. This gift of love shall
be the key which will unlock the storehouse for
you. You are blessed because of the love you give
forth. In coming days such blessings shall you have
that you will feel you have no more room in your
heart to receive them. Go now to the tasks that
await your hands and I will work with and through
you as you fulfill your daily portion of work.

TWO STEPS

My Beloved, when you come into My Presence, open yourself wholly to Me, the Giver and sustainer of all Life. Drink deep of my Beloved fullness, blend your entire being with that great completeness of the Christ knowledge. Wait quietly for the words of wisdom which shall fall upon your inner ear, the ear of the soul. That soul both listens and speaks, for My child it is all one. Often the words you hear must needs be words of reproof, of warning, or of gentle command, but as you are filled with the spirit of the Christ, they shall more and more be words of love which you shall hear. Then shall your days be filled with love, overflowing. There will be duties for your hands to do as you walk the path with Me. You shall ever hold out a helping hand to others to whom I will direct you. Again I say, open yourself completely to Me. Then as you go forth from this sacred meeting, close the little door of your heart. Keep the sweetness of our communion locked within, that it may perfume your life. Close out the outer, close out all discord, close out all that is not of Me. Then shall you be able to walk the streets, and do your work among men, with glistening garments. Your world will be a world of light, for you shall carry aloft that light which never dims, outshining the very sun of the heavens. You can touch and cleanse and burn free the lives you contact, but these contacts can never dim your light, nor soil the glistening garments of your soul. So you see how necessary are these two steps: first the opening to Me, the Divine light, and second the closing away all that is of the world. Now let us be still, holding our sweet communion, then go forth to serve, never forgetting that the One you worship is mindful of you. His ear ever listens for your word of praise and love and adoration. Then indeed shall only love and adoration come into your life, and crown your days.

THE CANDLE OF THE LORD

My Beloved, keep yourself as the clear crystal cup, holding the lighted candle of your Lord. At the base of the flame there is a blue light and as it rises higher and higher it becomes golden and of such high vibratory quality, that it is just a pure ray of golden light. So shall it be with you. As you rise higher and higher in Christ consciousness you shall be enveloped by the pure ray of My love. You, yourself shall not see, nor fully realize the sheer beauty or purity of that ray which burns about you. As the candle burns so brightly within the crystal cup, that it seems not to be the candle burning at all, so shall the personal self of you be so blended with the rays of My presence that it shall be as nothing. Those who come into your presence will wonder at the glow you carry and will seek to know from whence it comes, and through you, they shall be led to find the divine flame within their own souls. So shall you fulfill your mission, as you go quietly along your way. Leave the course of your life and its development to Me. Only know yourself to be but the crystal cup, holding the lighted candle of your Lord.

THE FLAME

It is the flame which gives beauty to the candle which, without it, would be but wax. Likewise it is the flame of my spirit that gives beauty to the physical form. As you come to know the reality and beauty of this flame, you shall cultivate it within you, ever watching and praying that it burn steady and with a golden beauty. You shall make your body the clear crystal cup, in order that the flame may shine forth, a light for all to be guided by, who are walking in sense darkness.

How little you realize the power which you carry with you. It shall lead you on and up the path. It shall flood your being, burning through all circumstances and conditions. All things shall be lighted for you by My high flame of love. Feed this flame, keep it bright, and pure—this flame of pure spirit. Then indeed shall you walk the streets with My sign upon you. All those whom you contact will be lifted up in consciousness. Then indeed shall you truly be but the crystal cup, holding the lighted candle of the Lord.

DO NOT NEGLECT

As you dwell consciously in the warmth of My Presence, as we abide for a few moments in quiet meditation together, you shall take on the glory of your Lord. All else shall seem to fall away from you. While without the gentle rain washes the earth, bringing back the green to the hills, and when soon the colors of the spring flowers shall warm the darkest corners, so shall these few moments with Me, Beloved of my Heart, wash, refresh and renew your spirit, filling with bloom its waste places. I have many lessons for you, but your ear is holden and My words are unheeded through the busy hours of the day. Again I plead gently with you to never allow this time of our complete oneness to be forgotten in the busy rush of less important matters. If you will take note, you will find that always sometime each day there are a few moments given you when you have opportunity to listen to My directing voice and speak with Me. This time may be on the busy street, far from the altar where we often hold our communion. But you can light the candles on the altar of your heart and blend yourself consciously with the Giver and Sustainer of all life. Then shall I be able to truly bless your day, taking over all of its affairs, and your life shall move forward, swiftly in harmony, and in law and order. These are not idle words which I give to you, but words which you are to heed, and follow, in order that your life may have its fullness of living and service to Me.

BUILD FIRST WITHIN

Realize that all there is without must first be within you. Unless you have the consciousness of the beauty of a tree, or field or mountain, can there be any beauty for you? Unless you have the consciousness of love, can any one be lovely for you?

As you hold me in full, complete consciousness, to that degree will the glow of my Presence overflow all your outer experiences. So close and warm within you do you feel me this morning. Yea, I am awakening in your consciousness as never before. Great miracles shall take place for you, miracles in the sense that you in your old state of consciousness would never have dreamed possible. Nor would they have been possible, for only as you contact me, the One-all-together-lovely, can these blessings spring into manifestation for you and yours.

And so you dwell this day under the shadow of my protection, and truly do you abide in the secret place of the Most High.

YOU AND YOUR BELOVED

You go quietly about the duties of your day, engulfed so completely in Me, the one who is all love, that everywhere you go or whatever you do, it shall all be lovely. When the eye is single to Me, to the spirit of all loveliness, how can aught but what is lovely enter into its vision? Neither need you worry for your strength, for I am all strength to do what I desire to do through you. So likewise am I all wisdom. Shall I who formed the universe, swinging the planets into space, lack wisdom to meet the problems of your tiny day? Function so completely from your God-center that you will need give no thought to the day before you. Your only thought need be that of loving and praising Me for My wisdom and strength which do enfold and bless you. When twilight gently falls, peace and quietness shall fill your heart. You will give a sigh of contentment as you rest yourself with Me, knowing that all day we have walked and talked together, even as now we are quiet together. Twilight or sunrise, morning or night, nothing can separate you from the Lover of your soul. Time and distance play no part, for we are One, inseparable, you and your Beloved.

CLEANSE YOURSELF

You have but to allow Me to smile through your eyes, to speak through your voice. Allow My healing force to pour through your hands. Then shall all the Glory of the Father be a living fire about you. Nothing that happens in the outer realm shall penetrate that holy flame. You shall dwell as a thing set apart, even as one of the candles in the Holy temple shall you be guarded. As you express the Life of your being to all you meet, great floods of power shall pour into you again, and you shall walk and not be weary, run and faint not. So open yourself, cleanse yourself, that I, the Lord of your soul, shall manifest My Glory through you, My human vessel of expression.

SEE ONLY THE TRUTH

You, My Child, are functioning at the point of consciousness which you recognize in others. There-fore if to you they seem to function in illness, fear, grief or distress, that is the point of your consciousness, for there is truly only One to function. Therefore you must not see that which you do not wish to come to pass. As you look at the lives about you, know only Truth, the Truth and reality which is of Me, no matter what the seeming outer circumstances. Then shall healing flow from your garments. Then shall your words go forth in mighty power. Your own life shall be blessed and likewise all lives that dwell even for a moment in your thought. They shall be freed from that which binds them in mortal limitation.

This lesson is a jewel I give to you. Wear it in your crown and it shall glow with beauty, light, and power for you to use to lighten and glorify the darkest corners of earth plane consciousness.

CLASP MY HAND

My Beloved, weary is the way and thick the underbrush through which your feet struggle when you try to tread the path alone. You think that for a time you walk alone but even then I am there, silent though I must remain. You cannot by any will of yours separate yourself from Me, the living force within you. Give pause and heed well these words. As a little child pulls away from the mother's guiding hand, thinking to run across the lawn alone, so do you withdraw yourself from

Me. But the mother only steps back a step, and is still there waiting to catch and hold the little form when the steps falter. So do I, My Child. I am ever there—waiting,—watching,—guarding closely, yea even longing for the moment when you shall again recognize My presence and feel your need of Me. Then shall you once more clasp My hand held out so lovingly to you and we shall go on together in a blessed fellowship, down life's highway.

THE NEW YEAR

As the portals of the New Year swing wide for you, enter quietly with Me. Without there may be the screech of sirens and the blare of horns and trumpets. Within the heart of you is stillness and peace.

I speak to you, and My voice is low and soft. New days lie before you. New joys, new duties lie close at hand. Fear not to enter the unknown with Me, fear not to meet the coming days. Together in blessed fellowship we shall make each day a day of victorious living. You shall grow strong with My strength, brave with the assurance of My power and tender with the sweetness of My love.

When again the curtain falls on a year that is past, you shall smile into My eyes and say, "It was good, Lord, for it was lived in the consciousness of your Presence." So shall you go gladly forth, again, to meet the new days of the coming years.

PEACE

Over the entire earth plane, there is disturbance. It is as if an ant hill had been disturbed. Men run hither and thither, seeking satisfaction, seeking release. Yet, through this period of tumult there runs a thread of pure gold. This thread is the Truth of man's Being, his Oneness with Divinity.

You must seek out this golden thread. See it through all the tangled web of human weaving. Only as you do, shall Peace come to abide in your heart. And only as Peace abides in the heart of each, can it cover the land.

Beloved, seek this Peace. Seek to be still within. Be not disturbed at the outer picture. Your life will be encompassed by your consciousness of law and order, by love and the fulfilling of the virtues.

So be at Peace, My children. You shall stand as if upon a high mount, and the hectic rush shall not disturb you, and the Peace that passeth understanding shall be yours now and forever more.